D0932536

Palace of Versailles
Home to the Kings of France

Jennifer Howse

www.av2books.com

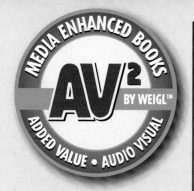

AV² provides enriched content that supplements and complements this book. Weigl's AV² books strive to create inspired learning and engage young minds in a total learning experience.

Your AV² Media Enhanced books come alive with...

Audio
Listen to sections of the book read aloud.

Key Words
Study vocabulary, and complete a matching word activity.

Video
Watch informative video clips.

Quizzes
Test your knowledge.

Go to **www.av2books.com**, and enter this book's unique code.

Embedded Weblinks
Gain additional information for research.

Slide Show
View images and captions, and prepare a presentation.

BOOK CODE

Q 5 7 3 5 4 3

Try This!
Complete activities and hands-on experiments.

AV² by Weigl brings you media enhanced books that support active learning.

... and much, much more!

Published by AV² by Weigl
350 5th Avenue, 59th Floor
New York, NY 10118
Websites: www.av2books.com   www.weigl.com

Library of Congress Cataloging-in-Publication Data

Howse, Jennifer.
 Palace of Versailles / Jennifer Howse.
   pages cm. -- (Castles of the World)
 Includes bibliographical references and index.
 ISBN 978-1-4896-3400-9 (hard cover : alk. paper) -- ISBN 978-1-4896-3401-6 (soft cover : alk. paper) -- ISBN 978-1-4896-3402-3 (single user ebk.) -- ISBN 978-1-4896-3403-0 (multi-user ebk.)
 1. Château de Versailles (Versailles, France)--Juvenile literature. 2. France--Kings and rulers--Dwellings--Juvenile literature. 3. Versailles (France)--Buildings, structures, etc.--Juvenile literature. I. Title.
 NA7736.V5H69 2015
 725'.1709443663--dc23
                        2015001367

Printed in the United States of America in Brainerd, Minnesota
1 2 3 4 5 6 7 8 9 0 19 18 17 16 15

032015
WEP070315

Editor: Heather Kissock
Design: Mandy Christiansen

Every reasonable effort has been made to trace ownership and to obtain permission to reprint copyright material. The publishers would be pleased to have any errors or omissions brought to their attention so that they may be corrected in subsequent printings. Weigl acknowledges Getty Images, Alamy, Corbis, iStock, and Dreamstime as its primary image suppliers for this title.

Contents

2 AV² Book Code
4 What Is the Palace of Versailles?
6 A Step Back in Time
8 The Palace of Versailles's Location
10 Outside the Palace
12 Inside the Palace
14 The Palace's Builders
16 Building the Palace
18 Similar Palaces around the World
20 Issues Facing the Palace
21 Design a Formal Garden
22 Palace of Versailles Quiz
23 Key Words/Index
24 Log on to www.av2books.com

What Is the Palace of Versailles?

France's Palace of Versailles stands as a **symbol** of a time when royalty held positions of power and privilege. Covering more than 2,000 acres (809 hectares) of land, the palace and its grounds showcase the luxurious lifestyles the kings and queens of France experienced in the 17th and 18th centuries. The palace's rooms are **gilded** with gold and lit with sparkling chandeliers. Its gardens are immaculately groomed. Master artworks line the palace hallways. Versailles demonstrates the height of royal splendor.

The French kings who built the Palace of Versailles were part of the Bourbon dynasty that ruled from 1589 to 1792.

The grandeur of the palace, however, also emphasizes the disparity between the social classes that existed at the time. This imbalance ultimately led to the fall of the French monarchy. In fact, a pivotal moment in the **French Revolution** took place at Versailles. In 1789, protestors stormed the palace and forced King Louis XVI and his wife, Marie-Antoinette, to move to Paris. Versailles ceased to be a royal residence from that point onward. Over the years, it has been home to government offices and a museum. Today, much of the palace has been restored to its former glory. It is now one of France's main tourist attractions.

More than 3 million people visit the Palace of Versailles every year.

The palace contains more than **700** rooms.

Versailles cost approximately **$2 billion** to build.

World War I formally ended at the palace, when the Treaty of Versailles was signed there in **1919**.

A Step Back in Time

The Palace of Versailles grew from modest beginnings. The first building to be constructed on the site was a hunting lodge, which was built for King Louis XIII. The site was chosen because it was surrounded by forests, which made the area perfect for hunting. When the king's son, Louis XIV, came to the throne, he decided to transform the site into a royal residence and move the French **court** from Paris to Versailles. This move brought the country's **nobility** to the countryside. Over the next two centuries, subsequent kings of France continued to add on to the palace, eventually creating the massive complex that exists today.

King Louis XIV oversaw four major building periods during his reign. Each added new buildings and gardens to the site.

1623–1624 A hunting lodge is built at Versailles for King Louis XIII.

1600	1625	1650	1670

1631 The hunting lodge is expanded to become a small **château**. The château completes construction in 1634.

1668 Le Vau begins the construction of the "enveloppe," a **façade** that faces the gardens and surrounds the original château.

1661 Louis XIV asks **architect** Louis Le Vau to expand upon the Versailles château. Construction begins on two new wings.

The Palace of Versailles is Baroque in design. This architectural style is known for being ornate and extravagant.

1671–1679 Two new wings are built to house various government officials and departments.

1770 The Royal Opera theater is completed to honor the marriage of the future King Louis XVI to Marie-Antoinette.

1979 Versailles is declared a UNESCO World Historical Site, making its **conservation** an international concern.

1675   1775   1900   2000

1833 King Louis-Philippe makes plans to create a museum at Versailles. It opens to the public in 1837.

1682 Versailles becomes the residence of King Louis XIV and the seat of the government. Construction begins on the Grand Commun, the living quarters for the palace's domestic staff.

1699 Construction begins on the palace chapel. It is completed in 1710.

The Palace of Versailles's Location

The Palace of Versailles is located about 10 miles (16 kilometers) southwest of Paris. When the palace first began construction, Versailles was a small village near the construction site. Now, it is a small city, with a population of more than 85,000 people. Besides being home to the palace, Versailles is also known as an administrative center, serving as the capital city of France's Yvelines **département**.

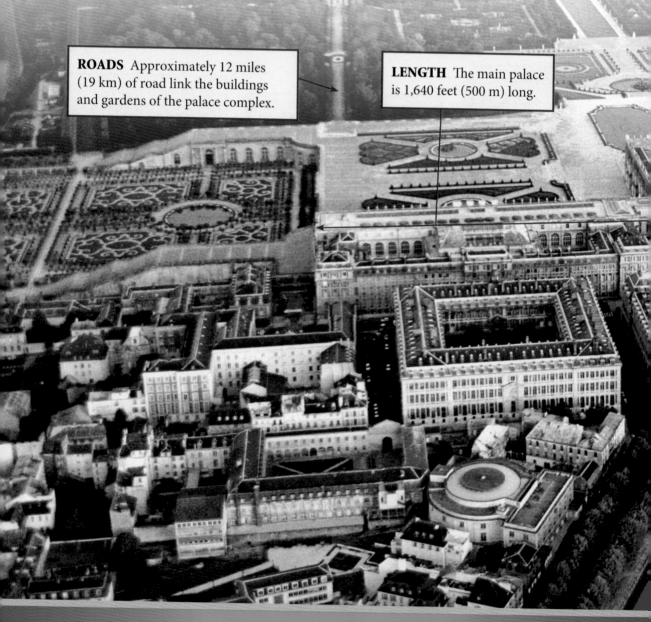

ROADS Approximately 12 miles (19 km) of road link the buildings and gardens of the palace complex.

LENGTH The main palace is 1,640 feet (500 m) long.

The palace complex is situated in the center of the city and is made up of several buildings. As well as the main palace, the site also has two smaller royal residences. The Grand Trianon was a private **retreat** built for King Louis XIV. He stayed there when he wanted to escape the rigors of court life. The Petit Trianon was the queen's private residence and was used for the same purpose. To the east of these small palaces was a small hobby farm called the Queen's Hamlet. Marie-Antoinette used the farm as her country home. Its vegetable gardens, fruit orchards, and livestock supplied food for the people who lived at the palace.

PARK AND GARDENS The palace's parkland covers approximately 2,000 acres (800 ha). The gardens extend over nearly 250 acres (100 ha).

FLOOR AREA The main palace has 551,112 square feet (51,200 square meters) of floor space.

In the late 18th century, approximately 60,000 people lived in and around Versailles, making it the largest urban center in France at that time.

Outside the Palace

The opulence of the Palace of Versailles is apparent from the outside. The building itself is an imposing structure. The surrounding features emphasize the stature of its original inhabitants.

GATE OF HONOUR As in the past, most visitors to the palace today enter the grounds through the Gate of Honour. Located directly in front of the palace, the gate is attached to a long **wrought iron** fence. The gate and fence are covered with **gold leaf**. Adornments on the gate include several royal symbols, such as **fleurs-de-lis** and cornucopias. The top of the gate features a gold crest and crown, representing the kings of France.

COURTYARDS Inside the main gate is a series of courtyards that leads to the palace entrance. The first courtyard is the Ministers' Courtyard, named for the two government buildings that flank it on each side. The Royal Courtyard sits farther back, within the arms of the palace itself. This area used to be reserved for royal carriages. People exiting their carriages would step onto the Marble Courtyard before walking into the palace.

GARDENS Versailles's gardens extend out from the back of the palace. Created in the French style, the gardens are known for their immaculate grooming, with trees clipped into specific shapes, and flowers and other plants arranged into imaginative designs. The gardens feature other decorative elements as well, including fountains, sculptures, and a canal that is about 1 mile (1.6 km) long.

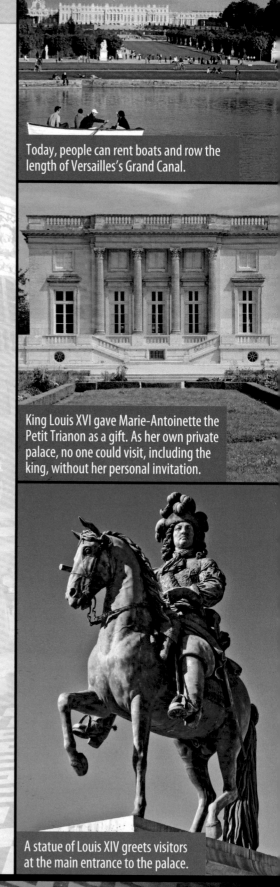

Today, people can rent boats and row the length of Versailles's Grand Canal.

King Louis XVI gave Marie-Antoinette the Petit Trianon as a gift. As her own private palace, no one could visit, including the king, without her personal invitation.

A statue of Louis XIV greets visitors at the main entrance to the palace.

The Marble Courtyard is named for the marble tiling that forms its floor.

The Orangerie gardens cover about 7.5 acres (3 ha) and feature a variety of fruit-bearing trees, such as orange, lemon, and pomegranate.

The current Gate of Honour is a replica of the original. The first gate was torn down during the French Revolution.

It took more than

40 YEARS

to create the palace gardens.

The Palace of Versailles was built to accommodate up to

5,000

people at a time.

The palace's stables could hold up to **2,000 horses.**

King Louis XIV often held boating parties in the Grand Canal.

The gardens feature
1,400
fountains
and more than
300
statues.

The Palace of Versailles has **2,143** windows.

1,250 brick chimneys run along the roofline of the palace.

Inside the Palace

The kings of France spared no expense when designing the palace interior. Rooms are decorated with luxurious fabrics, elaborate woodwork, and vivid artworks.

HALL OF MIRRORS The grandest room in the Palace of Versailles is the gleaming Hall of Mirrors, or Grande Galerie. Used as a passageway and reception room, the hall is 240 feet (73 m) long and contains 357 mirrors. These mirrors are held within 17 arches that run along the inside wall. Across from this wall are 17 corresponding windows. A series of chandeliers hang from the painted ceiling. During the 17th century, the hall was lit by candles and natural light. When the mirrors captured the light, the room sparkled with life.

ROYAL OPERA Planned by King Louis XIV and completed by King Louis XV, the Royal Opera theater was built in 1768 to host operas, ballets, and official royal functions. The theater can hold up to 1,336 spectators, and every seat has a good view of the stage. The building is made entirely of wood, which allows for excellent sound quality. In the past, 3,000 candles were required to light this large facility.

CHAPEL The chapel was built in the Baroque style, making use of its curving lines and rich colors. **Bas-reliefs** in white marble decorate the walls, arches, and pillars. The marble **inlaid** floors feature dramatic geometric designs. The chapel has two stories. The royal family sat in the top floor gallery when attending services.

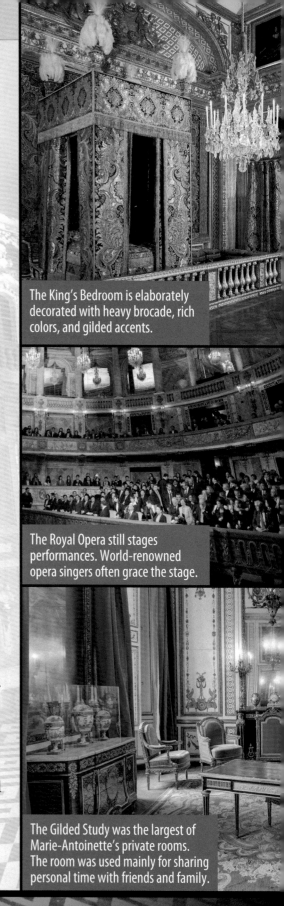

The King's Bedroom is elaborately decorated with heavy brocade, rich colors, and gilded accents.

The Royal Opera still stages performances. World-renowned opera singers often grace the stage.

The Gilded Study was the largest of Marie-Antoinette's private rooms. The room was used mainly for sharing personal time with friends and family.

As a convenience to the king, the upper gallery of the chapel was on the same floor as his private apartments.

Besides mirrors and chandeliers, the Hall of Mirrors also features statues and paintings.

One of Paris's rapid-transit trains has cars that have been painted to look like rooms in the palace.

On special occasions, the chandeliers in the Hall of Mirrors were lit with

20,000

candles, transforming the room into a corridor of light.

The Palace of Versailles has

67

staircases.

The palace houses at least

6,000

paintings and

2,000

sculptures.

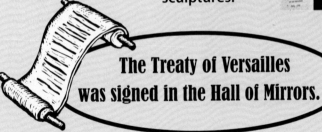

The Treaty of Versailles was signed in the Hall of Mirrors.

Some rooms in the palace have **secret** doors that open into hidden hallways.

The king's bedroom is situated in the **exact center** of the palace.

The Palace's Builders

Planning a palace as large as Versailles required vision and dedication. King Louis XIV had specific ideas for his new home, and it was the job of the architects, designers, and construction workers to make these ideas a reality. It is believed that more than 36,000 workers were involved in the construction of the palace.

Louis Le Vau Architect

Louis Le Vau was the palace's top architect. Born in Paris in 1612, Le Vau began his career by designing hotels and eventually graduated to larger projects. In 1654, he became the first architect to the king. Over the next few years, Le Vau worked on designs for the Louvre Museum and several other buildings. In 1667, he began developing the plans for Louis XIV's new palace. Le Vau was responsible for designing the royal apartments and the garden façade. Le Vau did not live to see the completion of the palace. He died in Paris in 1670.

Besides Versailles, Louis Le Vau was responsible for building homes for several high-ranking French politicians.

André Le Nôtre

Landscape Architect

André Le Nôtre was the designer of the palace's formal gardens. Born in 1613, Le Nôtre came from a long line of royal gardeners. After receiving architectural training from François Mansart, Le Nôtre succeeded his father as royal gardener at the Tuileries Palace in Paris. He began working on the Versailles gardens in 1662, gradually transforming the grounds into an incredible spectacle of green space. His work brought him much acclaim, and he was soon being invited to design gardens in cities across Europe.

André Le Nôtre's garden designs are still maintained and celebrated at Versailles.

Jules Hardouin-Mansart Architect

Jules Hardouin-Mansart took over the design and construction of Versailles in 1675. Hardouin-Mansart was born in Paris in 1646 and received his architectural training from his uncle, François Mansart. By the time Hardouin-Mansart was 30 years old, he was designing buildings for the king. He became royal architect in 1675 and was named chief architect to the king in 1681. Hardouin-Mansart was responsible for designing the Hall of Mirrors and the palace's north and south wings.

In 1693, Louis XIV gave Jules Hardouin-Mansart the title Chevalier of Saint-Michel in honor of his artistic contributions to the country.

Stonemasons

Stonemasons are specially trained to cut and shape rock into a desired form and install it properly on a structure. When working on the Palace of Versailles, they were responsible for cutting and shaping the stone that formed the palace's courtyards, exterior walls, and floors. Stonemasons must understand the **composition** of a stone block before they begin cutting it. They must also understand the grain of the stone and how to keep the stone from crumbling as they work it into the desired shape.

Today, stonemasons are in demand on restoration projects, helping to repair older buildings and cobblestone roads.

Landscape Gardeners

Landscape gardeners helped bring André Le Nôtre's ideas to life. Following his plans, they used flowers, trees, rocks, and fountains to make the gardens look beautiful. Landscape gardeners perform many tasks. They plant trees and flowers, build rock gardens, and mow grass lawns. They even create fountains and ponds for people to enjoy. Landscape gardeners often need to use local plants in their designs, so they must have a good understanding of **botany**.

Landscape gardeners work in a variety of settings, ranging from residential gardens to playgrounds and golf courses.

Laborers

Laborers contributed much to the actual construction of the palace. They helped clear the site and prepare it for construction. They then hauled materials to the construction site and helped place them into position on the building. Laborers continue to play an important role in construction today. They perform many jobs, including cleaning sites, loading materials, and operating equipment.

Most laborers know how to use saws and other power tools.

Building the Palace

It was important to the French kings that the Palace of Versailles showcase their power and status. The size of the palace was important, but they also wanted to make sure that it was equipped with the latest technologies and the best materials. Much effort was put into creating a royal residence that surpassed all others at the time.

LIVING IN LUXURY In the 1600s and 1700s, most people did not have the luxury of hot and cold running water. If they needed water, they would take large pots and gather it from a main water source. If the water had to be hot to take a bath or do laundry, they had to heat it themselves over a fire. When King Louis XV came to the throne, he wanted his water to be easily accessible, so he had the building's designers plan a system that allowed water to run into his apartments through pipes and taps. A water heating system ensured that he had hot water when he needed it. This same heating system was also used to provide heat in the palace rooms.

GROWING THE GARDEN Maintaining gardens the size of those at Versailles required an innovative approach and considerable planning. To ensure the gardens received the water they needed, the landscape architect had to develop irrigation plans. Water was diverted from nearby rivers and directed into the palace's gardens through a network of **aqueducts** and water pumps. While aqueducts had been in use for centuries, the water pump system was a new technology created specifically for the palace gardens. Much of the water was used to keep the ground moist, but it was also put on display in the palace's fountains. To make the water stream upward and outward, engineers designed a **hydraulics** system, which used pressure to force the water into the air.

A GOLD LINING From gateways to furniture, gold is a major decorative accent at the Palace of Versailles. Gold is one of the most **malleable** metals. It can be easily pounded into thin sheets to make gold plating. Gold can be used on the exterior or interior of buildings as a long-lasting covering. This is because it does not **corrode** or break down like other metals. Gold plating was used throughout Versailles not only to demonstrate the king's wealth, but because it could face all kinds of conditions, including wind, rain, snow, and sunlight, without being degraded.

At first, heated water was only available in two of Versailles's bathtubs, as well as the sunken pool found in the king's apartments.

Adding to the glitter of the Hall of Mirrors are the gilded statues that hold the floor lighting.

The Latona Fountain is Versailles's most recognized fountain. The water stored underneath it is distributed to all of the palace's other fountains.

Innovation also extended into the Royal Opera. For parties and other events, the orchestra pit could be raised to create a dance floor.

Similar Palaces around the World

Versailles was built as a place to show the importance of France and the significance of French royalty. The palace had a great influence on other European monarchs. Wanting to demonstrate the status of the crown in their own countries, many followed the lead of Louis XIV and built their own palatial homes. These buildings displayed the wealth and prestige of their inhabitants while also serving as **diplomatic** centers.

Grand Peterhof Palace

BUILT: 1714–1725, and 1746–1755 AD
LOCATION: Saint Petersburg, Russia
DESIGN: Jean-Baptiste-Alexandre Le Blond, Francesco Bartolomeo Rastrelli
DESCRIPTION: Russia's Tsar Peter the Great had been in the process of building a new palace when he paid a visit to the French court and saw Versailles. He promptly decided that his new palace should be in the same style. Like Versailles, the Grand Peterhof Palace was to have large gardens and its own canal. Construction stopped when the tsar died in 1725, but resumed under the reign of his grandaughter, Elizabeth. Under her watch, the palace was expanded to include another story, a new wing, and a small church. Today, people stand in awe at the size of the palace and its lavish interior, which includes ceiling murals, crystal chandeliers, and gilded statues.

The Grand Peterhof Palace is often called the "Russian Versailles." Today, it is a museum that showcases the life of Russian royalty in the 1700s.

Palácio Nacional de Queluz

BUILT: 1747–1786 AD
LOCATION: Queluz, Portugal
DESIGN: Mateus Vicente de Oliveira, Jean-Baptiste Robillon, Manuel Caetano de Sousa
DESCRIPTION: Commissioned by Portuguese King Pedro III, the Palácio Nacional de Queluz was built to serve as a private residence for the royal family of Portugal. Often referred to as the "Portuguese Versailles," the palace features architectural styles from three different eras. Its interior features include mirror-lined walls and gilded woodcarvings. Outside, the palace is surrounded by gardens, which are decorated with statues, fountains, and tiled pathways.

While the palace is a popular tourist site in Portugal, it still serves an official function. It is often used to accommodate visiting heads of state. Several American presidents have stayed there.

Royal Palace of Herrenchiemsee

BUILT: 1878–1886
LOCATION: Chiemsee, Bavaria, Germany
DESIGN: Georg von Dollmann
DESCRIPTION: The Bavarian version of Versailles was built on the orders of King Ludwig II of Bavaria following a visit to Versailles. Similar to the Palace of Versailles, the Herrenchiemsee Palace has a grand King's Bedroom and sweeping main staircase. Herrenchiemsee also features its own Hall of Mirrors. At a length of 320 feet (98 m), it is more than 80 feet (24 m) longer than the hall at Versailles. Although the palace was not completed due the early death of King Ludwig, it is an excellent example of Baroque design.

The Royal Palace of Herrenchiemsee is located on an island in the middle of Lake Chiemsee. It is accessible by ferry.

Issues Facing the Palace

The Palace of Versailles has experienced much turmoil in its history. After the royal family was forced from the palace, the buildings were almost destroyed by angry citizens. Restoration work did not begin until the 1800s. Today, **conservators** continue this work in an effort to return the palace to its original condition.

WHAT IS THE ISSUE?

Heavy tourist traffic creates stress on the buildings and its contents.	France can be susceptible to severe storms.

EFFECTS

The building's art and artifacts are exposed to dust and the light from camera flashes. Floors lose their finish as people walk over them.	In 1999, a wind storm destroyed more than 10,000 of the trees on the palace grounds. About 80 percent of the trees were rare species.

ACTION TAKEN

The palace is closed on Mondays to allow for cleaning and conservation efforts. Floors are waxed, and dust is removed from statues, paintings, and other artifacts.	The government decided to use this tragedy as an opportunity. A replanting campaign began to replace the fallen trees and to upgrade the gardens. To date, 50,000 new trees have been planted.

Design a Formal Garden

Imagine that you have been hired to design a formal garden. You have been given free rein to create the garden however you want, but have been told that it must have four distinct sections and contain flowers, trees, statues, and at least one fountain. Plan your garden following the steps below.

Materials
- Sheet of paper
- Ruler
- Pencil
- Colored markers or pencils

Instructions

1. Measure the paper lengthwise with the ruler. Mark the exact center of the paper on each side. Join these points by drawing a line across the paper. Turn the paper, and repeat the process on the width side. The paper should now be divided into four even squares.

2. Decide on a theme for each of the four garden squares. You can select themes based on stories you have read, your hobbies, or any of your other interests. Write your theme at the top of each square.

3. Keeping these themes in mind, begin to plan the design of each garden square. Decide where the pathways will be and where the trees and flowers will go. Which garden will be best for the fountain? What kinds of statues will each garden have? Map each garden's features in the appropriate square.

4. Use the markers to show how colorful your garden will be. When complete, hang the paper on your wall or refrigerator for your friends and family to see.

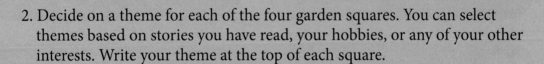

Palace of Versailles Quiz

Q How many rooms does the Palace of Versailles have?

A More than 700

Q Who designed the gardens at the Palace of Versailles?

A André Le Nôtre

Q What kind of building did Louis XIII originally have constructed at Versailles?

A A hunting lodge

Q How long is the Hall of Mirrors?

A 240 feet (73 m)

Key Words

aqueducts: channels designed to transport water from a remote source

architect: a person who designs buildings

bas-reliefs: the projections of figures from a flat surface, as in sculpture

botany: the study of plants

château: a large French country house or castle

composition: the way that something is made up

conservation: the preservation and protection of a place or object

conservators: people who protect objects from deterioration

corrode: to wear away gradually

court: the family and associates of a monarch

département: a major branch or subdivision of the French government

diplomatic: involved in maintaining good relations between the governments of different countries

façade: the principal front of a building

fleurs-de-lis: stylized lilies found on France's former coat of arms

French Revolution: an uprising that took place in France from 1789 to 1799, which eventually brought down the monarchy

gilded: covered with a thin layer of gold

gold leaf: gold plate that has been applied to a surface

hydraulics: operated by the pressure of fluid

inlaid: set something into a surface as decoration

malleable: can be stretched or bent into different shapes

nobility: a social class containing people who have more privileges than others

retreat: a place of privacy

symbol: an image which represents an idea or thing

wrought iron: a form of iron that is tough but malleable

Index

chapel 7, 12, 13
courtyards 10, 11, 15

fountains 10, 11, 15, 16, 17, 19, 21
French Revolution 5, 11

gardens 4, 6, 8, 9, 10, 11, 14, 15, 16, 18, 19, 20, 21, 22
Gate of Honour 10, 11
Grand Canal 10, 11
Grand Peterhof Palace 18
Grand Trianon 9

Hall of Mirrors 12, 13, 14, 17, 19, 22
Hardouin-Mansart, Jules 14
hunting lodge 6, 22

King Louis XIII 6, 22
King Louis XIV 6, 7, 9, 10, 11, 12, 14, 18
King Louis XVI 5, 7, 10

Le Nôtre, André 14, 15, 22
Le Vau, Louis 6, 14

Marie-Antoinette 5, 7, 9, 10, 12

Palácio Nacional de Queluz 19
Petit Trianon 9, 10

Queen's Hamlet 9

Royal Opera 7, 12, 17
Royal Palace of Herrenchiemsee 19

Treaty of Versailles 5, 13

Log on to www.av2books.com

AV² by Weigl brings you media enhanced books that support active learning. Go to www.av2books.com, and enter the special code found on page 2 of this book. You will gain access to enriched and enhanced content that supplements and complements this book. Content includes video, audio, weblinks, quizzes, a slide show, and activities.

AV² Online Navigation

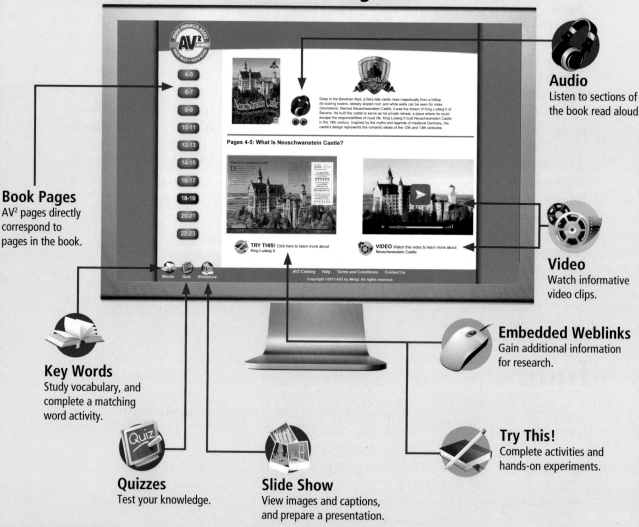

Audio
Listen to sections of the book read aloud

Book Pages
AV² pages directly correspond to pages in the book.

Video
Watch informative video clips.

Key Words
Study vocabulary, and complete a matching word activity.

Embedded Weblinks
Gain additional information for research.

Quizzes
Test your knowledge.

Slide Show
View images and captions, and prepare a presentation.

Try This!
Complete activities and hands-on experiments.

AV² was built to bridge the gap between print and digital. We encourage you to tell us what you like and what you want to see in the future.

Sign up to be an AV² Ambassador at www.av2books.com/ambassador.